THE NATURE KIDS GUIDE TO

WOMBATS

DAVID ANDERSON

LP Media Inc. Publishing
Text copyright © 2026 by LP Media Inc.
All rights reserved.

For information address LP Media Inc. Publishing,
30012 Variolite St NW, Princeton MN 55371
www.lpmedia.org

Publication Data

Wombats
The Nature Kid's Guide to Wombats — First edition.

Summary: "Learn all about Wombats, the Nature Kid Way"
— Provided by publisher.

ISBN: 979-8-89818-137-6

[1. Wombats – Non-Fiction] I. Title.

Title: The Nature Kid's Guide to Wombats

CONTENTS

BURROW BUILDERS

Scratch! A wombat digs in the dirt. Its strong claws push through soil.

Wombats live in **burrows**. These underground tunnels can stretch over 650 feet long! Inside, there are many rooms and paths.

Burrows stay cool and dark. This helps wombats escape the hot sun. They sleep underground during the day and come out at night.

Different wombats like different habitats. Common wombats live in forests with lots of trees. Southern hairy-nosed wombats prefer dry grasslands. Northern hairy-nosed wombats live in warm, sandy areas.

Wombats like soft soil for digging. But their strong claws can break through hard ground too.

DOWN UNDER

Tasmania is an island. It is south of Australia. Only common wombats live there.

Thump! A wombat waddles across dry land. This chunky animal lives in Australia.

Wombats live only in Australia. You will not find them anywhere else in the world!

Common wombats live along the east coast. They are found in mountains and forests from Queensland to Tasmania.

Southern hairy-nosed wombats live farther inland. They roam the flat, dry plains of South Australia.

Northern hairy-nosed wombats are the rarest. Only about 400 are left. They all live in one protected park in Queensland.

CHUNKY CHAMPS

Grunt! A round wombat sits in the grass. It looks like a small bear.

Wombats are chunky animals. They weigh between 44 and 77 pounds. That is about as heavy as the average dog!

These round creatures can grow to be about 3 feet long. Their bodies are low and wide. Short legs hold up their heavy frames.

The Northern hairy-nosed wombat is the largest kind of wombat. Southern hairy-nosed wombats tend to be a bit smaller and lighter.

A wombat's brain is small for its body size. It weighs only about two ounces!

BUILT
TOUGH

Crunch! A wombat chews tough roots. It takes a strong body to live this way.

Wombats have bodies made for digging. Their bones are thick and heavy. Strong muscles cover their shoulders and legs. Their claws are wide and powerful like shovels.

A wombat's skull is very hard and almost flat on top. This shape protects the brain while digging through dirt and rocks.

Their tough skin also helps protect them underground.

A wombat's front teeth never stop growing. Chewing tough roots wears them down!

SNIFF IT

Sniff! A wombat lifts its nose. It smells the night air.

Wombats have an amazing sense of smell. Their noses help them find food in the dark. They sniff out tasty roots and grasses underground.

Wombat eyesight is not very good. Their small eyes do not see well in bright light.

This does not matter much. Wombats are active at night. Their noses guide them through darkness.

FUN FACT!

Wombat poop is shaped like little cubes! They leave these squares on rocks and logs. Other wombats can smell who left it there.

BUM BLOCK

Stomp! A predator gets too close. The wombat backs up fast. It runs to its den.

Wombats have a secret weapon. Their backside is like armor! It has four hard plates covered in thick **cartilage** and skin.

When danger comes, wombats run to their burrows. They dive in headfirst. Then they block the door with their hard rumps.

This armor is very tough. Predators cannot bite through it. Some wombats even crush attackers against the tunnel roof!

Wombats can run up to 25 miles per hour in short bursts. They run this fast to escape danger!

DID YOU KNOW?

GRASS GRAZERS

Munch! A wombat nibbles on grass. Its flat teeth grind the plants.

Wombats eat mostly grasses. They also munch on roots, bark, and shrubs. Their teeth never stop growing. This helps because tough plants wear teeth down.

Wombats feed at night when it is cool. They graze for 3 to 8 hours each night.

These animals do not need much water. They get most of it from the plants they eat. Wombats can go for weeks without needing to drink!

It takes wombats 14 days to digest one meal!

GRUNT TALK

FUN FACT!
Wombats greet friendly neighbors with a cough-like sound. Sometimes they even squeal like a pig!

Hiss! A wombat makes a raspy sound. Another wombat listens nearby.

Wombats make many sounds. They hiss, growl, and make clicking noises. These sounds help them talk to other wombats.

Most wombats live alone. But they still need to communicate. A loud hiss tells another wombat to stay away.

Mothers and babies make soft sounds to each other. Young wombats use soft hissing sounds to call their mothers. Wombats also send messages without sound. They leave scent marks on rocks and logs.

WATCH OUT

Growl! A dingo walks near a burrow. A wombat hides inside.

Wombats have a few predators. Dingoes are their main threat. These wild dogs hunt wombats in Australia.

Tasmanian devils hunt wombats too. They live on the island of Tasmania. Wedge-tailed eagles are also a danger. They hunt young wombats.

Baby wombats face the most danger. They are small. They cannot run fast yet. Adult wombats are safer. They are big and strong.

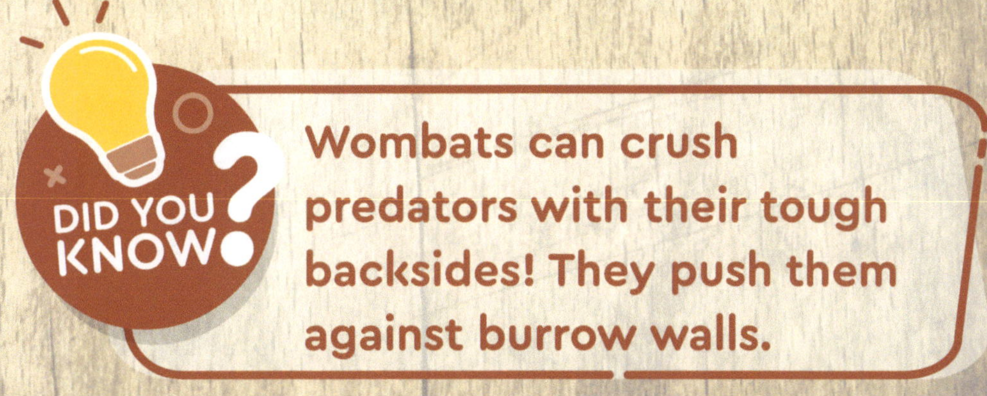

DIVE DEEP

Whoosh! A wombat runs into its tunnel. It goes underground.

Wombats dig fast. When danger comes, they dive into burrows. Their tunnels can be over 650 feet long!

Inside, wombats are safe. If a predator follows, the wombat blocks the entrance with its tough, bony bottom!

Some burrows have many exits. This helps wombats escape. They can pop out far from danger!

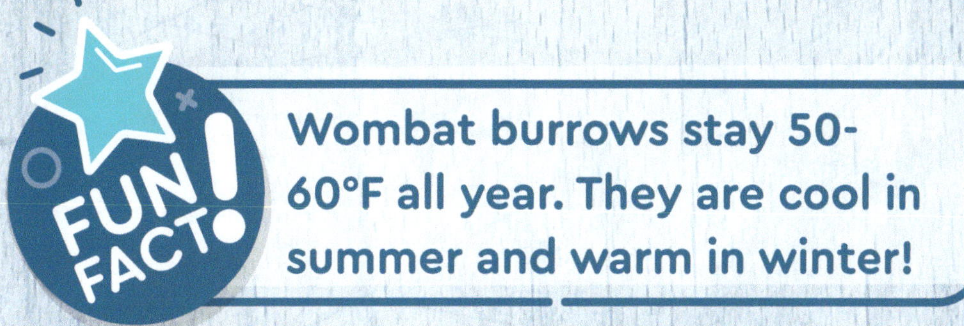

Wombat burrows stay 50-60°F all year. They are cool in summer and warm in winter!

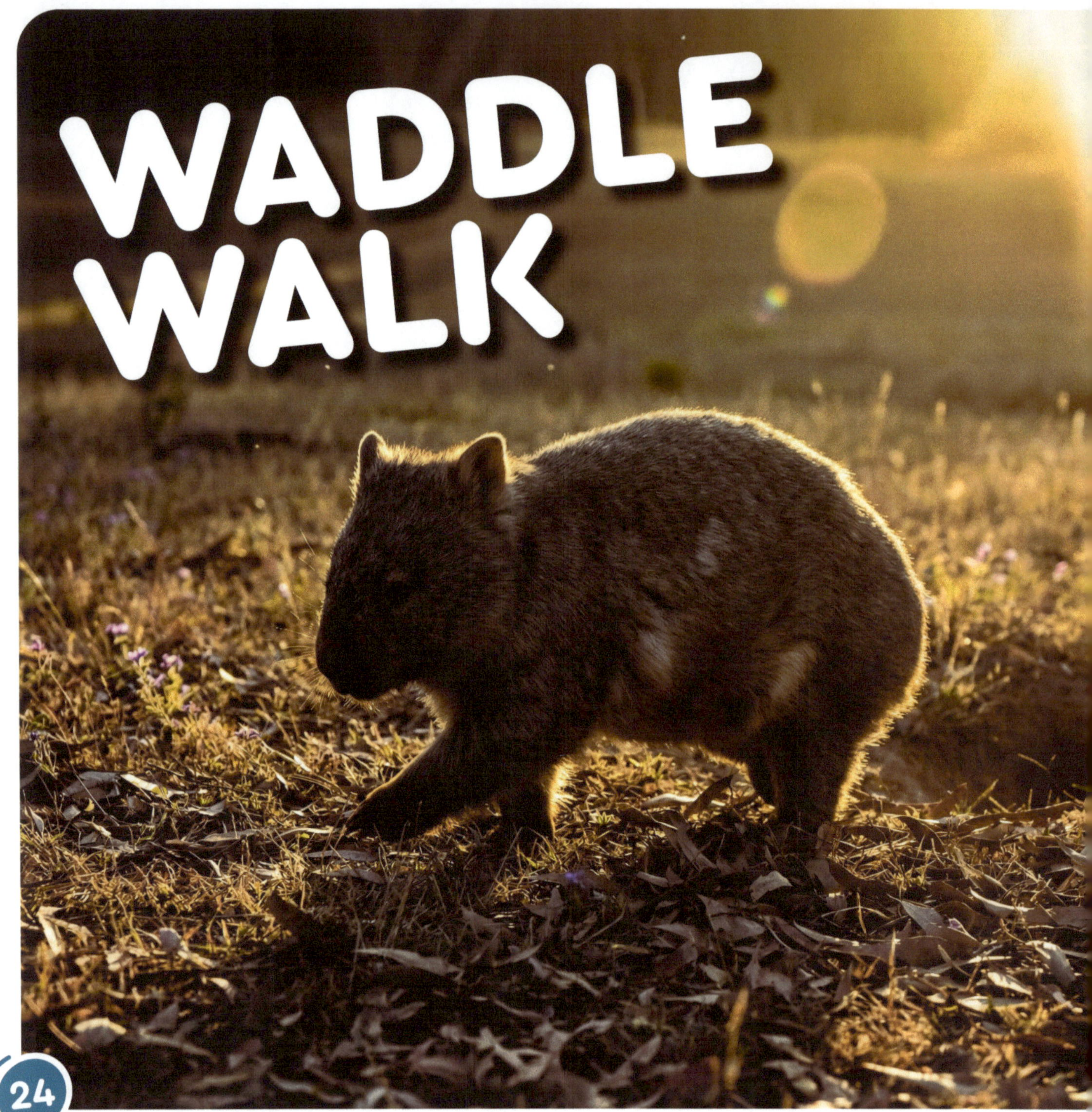

WADDLE
WALK

Rustle! A wombat walks through dry leaves at night.

Wombats waddle when they walk. Their short legs give them a swaying motion. They look slow and clumsy on land.

But wombats can run fast when needed! They can reach speeds up to 25 miles per hour when running from a predator.

When they run, they gallop like a horse. They can also turn very quickly to dodge danger.

Wombats walk on their toes, not flat-footed like most animals. This is called digitigrade.

NIGHT SHIFT

Yawn! A wombat wakes up at dusk. It is time to eat.

Wombats are **nocturnal**. This means they are active at night. They sleep during the hot daytime hours.

When the sun sets, wombats come out. They spend about 3 to 8 hours outside each night. Most of this time is spent eating grass.

Wombats come out at night because the air is cooler. They do not sweat. Staying in cool burrows by day keeps them safe.

Wombats can travel up to 2 miles in one night while looking for food and exploring their territory.

LONE WANDERERS

Shhh! A wombat walks alone. It sniffs the quiet night air.

Wombats are **solitary** animals. They live alone most of the time. Still, they often share their burrows with other wombats.

Wombats do not form herds or packs. They prefer to stay by themselves.

When wombats meet, they may sniff each other. Then they simply go their separate ways. They are happiest alone.

One wombat may have up to 12 burrows. Each burrow can stretch hundreds of meters long!

FINDING FRIENDS

Snort! A wombat sniffs a scent mark on a log. She is looking for a mate.

When it is time to have babies, wombats give up their solitary life and find a mate. Male wombats will follow scent trails to find females.

Once they find them the males chase the females in circles. They may bite gently at her sides. This playful chase can go on for many minutes.

Female wombats usually have one baby every two years.

Wombats usually mate in spring and summer. A female is pregnant for only 20 to 22 days!

TINY JOEYS

Squeak! A young joey peeks out from its mother's pouch.

A baby wombat is called a **joey**. It is born very tiny, about the size of a jellybean!

The joey crawls into its mother's pouch right after birth. Inside the pouch, it drinks milk and grows. It stays safe and warm there for about 6 to 10 months.

The pouch faces backward on a wombat. This keeps dirt out when the mother digs her burrow. What a clever design!

A newborn wombat joey weighs about 1 to 2 grams. That is lighter than a paperclip or a single raisin!

POUCH
POWER
34

Chirp! A mother wombat carries her joey safely in her pouch.

Mother wombats take good care of their babies. The joey stays in the pouch for about 6 to 10 months. It drinks milk and grows big and strong.

After leaving the pouch, the joey stays close to its mother. It follows her around and learns to find food, and learns to dig with its strong claws.

Mothers protect their joeys from danger. A joey may stay with its mother for up to two years. Then it is ready to live alone.

DID YOU KNOW

A mother wombat lines a nest with grass and leaves inside her burrow

TOUGH TUNNELERS

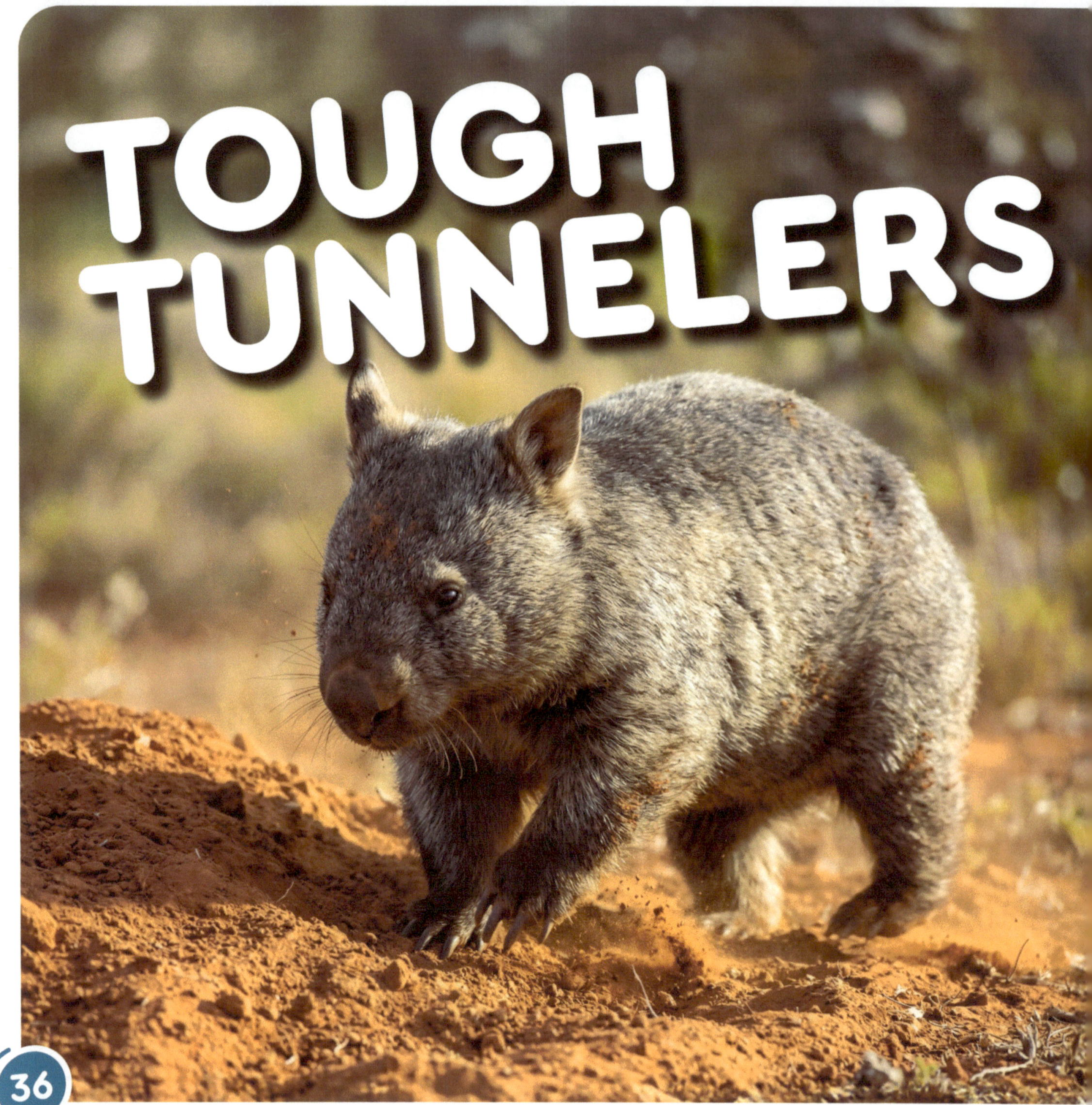

Dig! A wombat tunnels to safety. Wombats are survivors.

Wombats have lived in Australia for over 25 million years. Long ago, there were giant wombats that were as big as cars!

Australia became hotter and drier. Wombats adapted. They dug cool burrows to escape the heat. When food was scarce, they dug for roots. Their burrows kept them safe for millions of years.

The biggest giant wombat weighed as much as a cow! It was too big to dig burrows like wombats do today.

WOMBAT
WATCH

Shhh! A person watches a wombat. It is far away. The wombat nibbles grass.

Wombats are shy. They stay near their burrows. The best time to see them is at dawn. Dusk is good too. That is when they eat.

You can see wild wombats in Australia. But they also live in zoos across the world. Get to the zoo early, wombats usually nap during the day so the best chance to see them is in the morning or right before the zoo closes!

Maria Island is in Tasmania. It has no predators. So the wombats there are extra friendly!

GLOSSARY

burrows
Tunnels that animals dig underground to live in.

nocturnal
Active at night and sleeping during the day.

cartilage
A tough, bendy material in the body that is softer than bone.

solitary
Living alone instead of in a group.

joey
A baby wombat or other pouched animal.

www.ingramcontent.com/pod-product-compliance
Lightning Source LLC
Chambersburg PA
CBHW041622110726

48005CB00002B/472